GET BY IN SPANISH

**A quick beginners' course for
holidaymakers and businesspeople**

Course writer: Jane Freeland
Editor: Susan Stone
Producer: Christopher Stone
Executive Producer: Edith Baer

BRITISH BROADCASTING CORPORATION

Get by in Spanish
A BBC Radio course
First broadcast March 1977

Published to accompany a series of programmes prepared in consultation with the BBC Continuing Education Advisory Council

Published by
BBC Publications
a division of BBC Enterprises Ltd
35 Marylebone High Street
London W1M 4AA

ISBN 0 563 16257 0
First published in 1978. Reprinted 1979, 1981, 1982 (twice),
1983 (twice), 1984, 1985 (twice), 1986
© The Authors and BBC Enterprises 1978

Printed in England
by Belmont Press, Northampton
This book is set in 10 on 11 point Univers Medium

Contents

The course...and how to use it

Get by in Spanish is a five-programme radio course for anyone planning a visit to a Spanish-speaking country. It provides, in a short learning period, a basic 'survival kit' for situations typical of a visit abroad.

The programmes
- concentrate on the language you'll need to cope with a particular situation: meeting people, ordering food, asking the way, etc.,

- give you the opportunity of practising words and phrases aloud and answering simple questions,

- help you learn to pick out the key information so that you can get the gist of what people say,

- include real-life conversations with Spanish people to let you hear authentic Spanish right from the start.

The two cassettes contain the radio programmes in slightly shortened form and offer you the chance to study at your own pace.

The book includes the text of the conversations heard in the programmes, a summary of what has been taught, brief language notes, tips about daily life in Spain, and self-checking exercises. Some exercises are marked *; when you have done these they make up a conversation which you can check at the beginning of the next programme.

The underlined parts in the conversations show you the minimum you need to speak in order to 'get by'.

At the end of the book you'll find additional language notes, a pronunciation guide, a word list and a key to the exercises.

To make the most of the course

Everybody has a personal way of learning and much will depend on whether you're using the cassettes or following the radio broadcasts, or both. Here are some suggestions:

- Get used to the sound of Spanish by first listening to the programme without looking at the book. Concentrate on picking out clues. With the cassettes you may prefer to go through the programme in sections.

- During the practice sequences repeat aloud what you're asked to say. This will help you get your tongue round unfamiliar sounds and give you confidence in speaking. On the cassette tapes the pauses for your reply are timed to allow for a little thought but a fairly prompt answer. If the pauses seem too short at first lengthen them by stopping the machine. Continue practising until your answer fits the pause.

- After the programme go through the book chapter. Look up any words you don't know in the word list. Read the conversations, with someone else if possible. The pronunciation guide on p. 64 will help you with reading aloud. If you have the cassettes, check your pronunciation by imitating the speakers phrase by phrase (use the pause button to stop the tape).

- Go through the language summary and explanations. Then attempt the exercises.

- Before the next programme read through the chapter in advance.

Whichever method of learning you decide on the golden rule is to do a little and often.

When you go abroad take the book with you, plus a good pocket dictionary and a notebook to jot down words and expressions you discover for yourself.

If you can get by in Spanish you'll enjoy your visit all the more. *¡Buena suerte!*

1 Getting food and drink

Conversations

These conversations are included in the programmes.
Read them over as often as you can after you have
listened to the broadcasts or cassettes. If you have the
cassettes use them to check your pronunciation.

Before attempting the conversations you may prefer
to go through the language summary that follows.
Look up any words and phrases you don't know in
the word list on page 68.

The underlined parts are the absolute minimum you
need to be able to say to get by.

Meeting people

Señor	Buenos días. ¿Cómo está usted?
Señora	Buenos días. Muy bien, ¿y usted?
Señor	Muy bien, gracias.

Señor	Buenas tardes. ¿Cómo está usted?
Señora	Muy bien, muchas gracias. ¿Y usted?
Señor	Muy bien, gracias.

Being offered things

Eduardo	Hola, buenos días, María Antonia.
María Antonia	Hola, buenos días.
Eduardo	Siéntese. ¿Cómo está?
María Antonia	Muy bien, gracias. ¿Y usted?
Eduardo	Muy bien, gracias. ¿Un cigarrillo?
María Antonia	Sí, gracias.
Eduardo	¿Y un vaso de vino?
María Antonia	Sí, gracias.

siéntese *sit down*

Señor	¿Le gusta la paella?
Señora	Me gusta mucho.
Señor	¿Quiere más?
Señora	Sí, gracias.

Señor	¿Le gusta el vino?
Señora	Me gusta mucho.
Señor	¿Quiere un poco más?
Señora	No, gracias. Basta.
Señor	(*insistent*) ¿Un poco más?
Señora	No, basta, basta.

Getting attention and ordering

Señora	Por favor. ¡Oiga, por favor!
Camarero	Sí, señora. ¿Qué quiere?
Señora	Un café, por favor.
Camarero	Sí, señora. Ahora mismo.

ahora mismo   *right away*

Señora	¡Oiga, por favor!
Camarero	Buenos días. ¿Qué desea?
Señora	La carta, por favor. (*He hands it to her*)
Camarero	¿Qué quiere?
Señora	Éste, por favor.
Camarero	Éste – el bistec con ensalada. Muy bien.

el bistec con ensalada   *steak with salad*

Señora	Yo quiero una taza de té.
Camarero	¿Con limón o con leche?
Señora	Con leche, por favor.

una taza de té   *a cup of tea*

Language summary

Greetings
How to say 'hello' . . .

hola   *any time*

buenos días   *before lunch*

buenas tardes   *after lunch and in the early evening*

buenas noches   *late evening, at night*

and 'goodbye'

adiós

adiós, buenos días *etc.*

Saying 'how do you do?' . . .

¿cómo está (usted)? (*formal*)

(hola) ¿qué tal? (*informal*)

and answering 'fine thanks, and how are you?'

muy bien, gracias, ¿y usted?

(hola) ¿qué tal?

Hospitality
Being offered things...

¿taxi?
¿hotel?
¿un cigarrillo?
¿un vaso de vino?

and accepting

sí, gracias

muchas gracias

. . . or refusing

no, gracias

. . . and more things

¿más?
¿quiere más?

¿quiere más | paella?
                | café?
                | vino?

¿un poco más?

sí, gracias

no, gracias

un poco más, por favor

basta, gracias

Do you like it/the . . . ?

¿le gusta?

¿le gusta | la paella?
        | el café?

I like it (very much)

me gusta (mucho)

I don't like it

no me gusta

Getting attention

por favor
oiga, por favor

| señor
| señora
| señorita
| camarero

Ordering food and drink

What would you like?

¿qué quiere (usted)?
¿qué desea (usted)?

Tea, coffee, brandy, menu, this one please

un té con limón
un café, por favor
un coñac
la carta/el menú
éste, por favor

Explanations

el . . . la/un . . . una
You may have noticed these differences:

¿le gusta *el* café?   BUT   ¿le gusta *la* paella?
                           (do you like *the* . . . ?)
¿quiere *un* café?   BUT   ¿quiere *una* paella?
                           (do you want *a* . . . ?)

In Spanish, both people and things are divided into
masculine and feminine (= m. and f. in dictionaries).
There's no easy way of learning this. Try to remember
el/un (masc.) and *la/una* (fem.) as if they were part
of the word. You will be understood without either –
the person you are talking to will be listening for the
word that follows, so if you make a mistake it will not
interfere with understanding.

Vd . . . Vds

Usted (you) appears in brackets as it is not always used in more informal conversations. It is often just written *Vd.* Similarly *ustedes* (plural) is written *Vds.*

¿ . . . ?/¡ . . . !

In written Spanish questions are indicated by an upside-down question mark at the beginning as well as the normal question mark at the end of the question. It's the same with exclamations.

Exercises

Do all these exercises after listening to the programme. Those marked * are for checking by ear at the beginning of the next programme. There is a written key to the others, on page 66.

1   Fill in the appropriate greeting for the situation:

a   You've just come down to breakfast. Say good morning to the Spanish family sitting at the next table. ....

b   You've met María Antonia for coffee after lunch. Greet her. ....

c   You've spent the afternoon on the beach and have dropped into a café to meet your friends. Greet them.

....

d   You're meeting a business colleague for an 11 a.m. appointment. Greet him and ask him how he is. ....

....

e   You've had coffee with María Antonia. Say goodbye...

f You've had your drink at the café. Say goodbye to your friends. ....

g You're tired. You're going to bed. Say goodnight...

....

2 You're at the airport, waiting for friends to pick you up by car and take you to stay with them. Reply to the following offers:

a ¿Taxi, señor? ....

b ¿Hotel? ....

c ¿Restaurante? ....

d ¿Mozo? ....

Back at their house, you need black coffee to keep you awake after the flight, you're longing for a cigarette, and you know your host has excellent wine. Reply to the following offers:

e ¿Quiere café? ....

f ¿Café solo? ....

g ¿Un cigarrillo? ....

h ¿Quiere un vaso de vino? ....

It is all delicious. Tell your friends how much you like everything.

j ¿Le gusta el café? (*yes*)....................

k ¿Le gusta el vino? (*very much*) ....

....

l ¿Un poco más? (*no thanks, you've had enough*)

....

m ¿Le gusta la paella? (*very much*) ....

....

3* You've met Eduardo in a Madrid café. Reply to his questions.

Eduardo	Hola, buenas tardes.
Usted	....
Eduardo	¿Cómo está?
Usted	....
Eduardo	Muy bien, gracias. ¿Quiere un café?
Usted	(*yes, please*) ....
Eduardo	Un café pues, ¿solo, o con leche?
Usted	(*without milk*) ....
Eduardo	¿Le gusta Madrid?
Usted	(*yes, very much*) ....

4* This time, you're on your own, ordering a meal. First, call the waiter:

Usted	....
Camarero	¿Qué desea?
Usted	(*you'd like to see a list of the dishes*) ....
Camarero	¿La carta? Sí, un momento. (*he hands it to you, and you point to your choice*)
Usted	(*this one, please*) ....
Camarero	¿Éste? La paella. ¿Quiere algo más con la paella?
Usted	(*you'd like a glass of wine*) ....
Camarero	Muy bien. Ahora mismo.

Worth knowing

Greetings and Goodbyes

Hola – a casual greeting used any time.
Buenos días – in the morning, until lunch.
Buenas tardes – after lunch, until early evening.
Buenas noches – late evening, at night.
More casually, you'll hear people say *buenas* or *muy buenas*.

Buenos días etc. are often added after *adiós* – goodbye, e.g. *Adiós, buenas tardes.*
You'll hear other phrases added after *adiós*, e.g.
Adiós, hasta luego – . . . see you later.
Adiós, hasta mañana – . . . see you tomorrow.
Adiós, hasta mañana, si Dios quiere – . . . see you tomorrow, God willing.

It's usual to shake hands when you meet and when you leave, especially if the meeting is formal. Women often embrace and touch cheeks. Men will embrace old friends and pat each other on the back.

Saying 'thank you'

Gracias said on its own in reply to an offer is taken to mean 'no, thank you' – better to keep to *sí, gracias* or *no, gracias.*
Muchas gracias – thank you very much.
Basta, basta, gracias – that's enough, thanks. Your host may press you to have more than you really want, thinking you are refusing out of politeness.

Titles

señor – when addressing a man
señora – when addressing a married or older woman
señorita – for a young woman or girl

These titles are also used with people's surnames:
  Señor Delgado – Mr Delgado
  Señora Marcos – Mrs Marcos
  Señorita Pérez – Miss Pérez.

Getting attention

It is not considered rude to clap your hands and snap your fingers to attract attention in bars and restaurants. You'll sometimes hear people making a very effective *tss* sound too. It's more polite to call the waiter with *oiga, camarero.*

Por favor can be added after requests and orders – it makes questions less abrupt.

Bars and cafés

Spanish bars, cafés and *cafeterías* (snack bars) tend to open early and close late. They provide food and drink and children are welcome. You pay a little more for waiter service.

Drinks: Beer is served either by the bottle (*una botella* – 1/3rd litre; *un botellín* – 1/5th litre) or on draught (*cerveza de barril* or *una caña*).

Wine – the two best-known wines are *Valdepeñas* and *Rioja* (more expensive), and there is plenty of cheap, palatable wine (*tinto* – red; *blanco* – white). *Sangría* is a wine and fruit punch.

Spirits – there is a vast range. You get larger measures than in England and the prices of Spanish brand spirits and liqueurs are comparably lower.

Non-alcoholic drinks – fizzy drinks *con gas*; still drinks *sin gas*. You can get tea (usually made from tea bags) with milk or lemon; coffee is either black or with milk (*solo* or *con leche*) – you won't get coffee with cream.

Food: Many bars provide tasty little appetisers called *tapas* which are served with your pre-dinner drink. *Bocadillos* are Spanish-style sandwiches – *un sandwich* is a toasted sandwich. In *cafeterías* you can eat snacks like hot dogs (*perros calientes*) or hamburgers (*hamburguesas*). In restaurants you can buy a set-price meal (*el menú del día*) which includes bread, wine and service. The list of dishes (*la carta*) is the range of dishes the restaurant provides and is usually translated into English.

Leaving a tip: Unless service is included (*servicio incluido*) it is usual to leave a tip (10–15% of your bill) when you are served at table in cafés and restaurants, though less necessary if you eat or drink standing up at the bar. Even if service is included it is appreciated if you leave a few pesetas.

2 Getting your shopping done

Conversations

Asking if they have what you want

En el restaurante

Señora	¡Oiga, por favor!
Camarero	Sí, señora.
Señora	Una paella para cuatro, por favor.
Camarero	No hay paella, señora, lo siento.

lo siento *I'm sorry*

En la frutería

Empleado	No hay tomates, lo siento.
Señora	¿Hay melones?
Empleado	No hay melones.
Señora	¿Hay uvas?
Empleado	¿Uvas? No hay, lo siento. Hay naranjas, hay plátanos, hay manzanas.

Beginning of side two, cassette one

Paying the bill

En el restaurante

Señor	¡Oiga, por favor!
Camarero	¿Qué quiere, la cuenta?
Señor	Sí, por favor.
Camarero	Un momento.
Señor	¿Cuánto es?
Camarero	Son exactamente ochocientas noventa y tres pesetas. Ocho, nueve, tres. Muchas gracias.

un momento *just a moment*
son exactamente ochocientas noventa y tres pesetas *that's exactly 893 pesetas*

Ordering teas and coffees

En el café

Señor	Tres cafés – no, dos tés y un café.
Señorita	No, no, no, no. Un té y dos cafés.
Señor	Un té y dos cafés.
Señorita	Bien.

Buying postcards and stamps . . .

En el estanco

Señor	Buenos días.
Empleada	Buenos días.
Señor	¿Tiene usted postales de esta ciudad?
Empleada	Sí. Aquí están. ¿Quiere usted mirarlas?
Señor	Sí. (*he looks at them*) Me gustan mucho. Le voy a comprar tres.
Empleada	Muy bien.
Señor	¿Cuánto es?
Empleada	Cada postal cuesta tres pesetas. Son tres, seis, nueve pesetas en total.
Señor	¿Cuánto es el sello para Inglaterra?
Empleada	Cada sello vale diez pesetas. Aquí tiene usted sellos para tres postales.
Señor	Gracias.
Empleada	De nada.
Señor	Adiós.
Empleada	Adiós.

¿tiene usted . . . ?   *do you have . . . ?*
de esta ciudad   *of this city*
¿quiere usted mirarlas?   *would you like to look at them?*
le voy a comprar   *I'm going to buy*
¿cuánto es el sello para Inglaterra?   *how much is a stamp for England?*
aquí tiene usted sellos para tres postales   *here are stamps for three postcards*
de nada   *that's all right*

. . . **petrol**

En la estación de servicio

Empleado	Buenos días.
Señora	Buenos días.
Empleado	¿Quiere super?
Señora	Sí, por favor.
Empleado	¿Cuánto?
Señora	Lleno.
Empleado	¿Lleno?

Empleado	Buenos días.
Señora	Buenos días.
Empleado	¿Cuánto?
Señora	Diez litros, por favor.
Empleado	Diez litros. Gracias.

. . . **ham**

En la tienda de comestibles

Empleado	Buenos diás, señora. ¿Qué desea?
Señora	Jamón, por favor.
Empleado	Sí, señora. ¿Cuánto quiere?
Señora	Para cuatro personas, por favor.
Empleado	Para cuatro. Mmm, ¿vale?
Señora	Mmm, un poco más.
Empleado	¿Vale? ¿Quiere más?
Señora	No, gracias, basta. ¿Cuánto es?

. . . **fish**

En la pescadería

Pescadero	¿Quiere algo más?
Señora	¿Hay sardinas, por favor?
Pescadero	Pues, sí. ¿Cuánto quiere?
Señora	Para nueve personas.
Pescadero	¿Vale?
Señora	Menos, por favor.
Pescadero	Menos. . . . ¿Vale?
Señora	Un poco menos, por favor. Vale, vale.

. . . groceries

En la tienda de ultramarinos

Señora	Buenos días, señor. Deseo un poco de vino.
Empleado	Sí, señora. Ciento veinticinco pesetas el litro.
Señora	Ciento veinticinco pesetas el litro. Sí, pues, ¿me da usted dos litros, por favor?
Empleado	Gracias.
Señora	Un kilo de azúcar, un kilo de café.
Empleado	¿Algo más?
Señora	Un poco de fruta.
Empleado	Ah, fruta. Tenemos naranjas, tenemos plátanos, manzanas, uvas.
Señora	Muy bien.
Empleado	¿Algo más, señora?
Señora	No, gracias. ¿Me da usted la cuenta, por favor?
Empleado	Sí, señora.

¿me da usted . . . ? *can I have . . . ?*
¿algo más? *anything else?*
tenemos naranjas . . . *we have oranges . . .*

Language summary

How to ask what's available

Is there any . . ./a . . . ?		*There is/there isn't any . . .*	
¿hay	paella?	hay	paella
	café?		café
	tomates?		tomates
	naranjas?	no hay	naranjas
	melones?		melones

Asking for more than one thing

What would you like?	*1, 2, 3, . . .* (full list of numbers on page 63)

¿qué quiere (usted)? ¿qué desea (usted)?	un té dos sellos tres postales cuatro melones cinco cafés

Asking the price

How much is it?	*. . . pesetas*
	cuatro pesetas trescientas pesetas *etc.*

	. . . pesetas each
¿cuánto es?	tres pesetas │ cada uno │ cada sello

	. . . pesetas a kilo/ litre/half a kilo etc.

	diez pesetas │ el kilo
	              │ el litro
	              │ el medio kilo

Saying how much you want

How much do you want?	*. . . kilo(s)/litre(s)*
¿cuánto quiere (usted)?	un kilo medio litro dos kilos tres litros

For how many people?	*for . . . (people)*

¿para cuántas personas?	para │ dos
	     │ cinco │ (personas)
	     │ nueve

Is this right/enough?	*(a bit) more/less, enough, OK*
¿vale?	(un poco) más/menos
¿basta?	basta, vale

Explanations

¿hay?

You'll have heard people saying:

un poco de	jamón/fruta
un litro de	leche/vino
un kilo de	azúcar/café

You can try using the whole phrase. More simply you can ask *¿hay vino?* or *¿hay jamón?* and wait to be asked *¿cuánto quiere?.* Then you can give the quantity separately.

Plurals

To make nouns plural, you add *-s*, when they end in a vowel: *-es*, when they don't:

| seis | personas
sellos
tomates | dos | melones
postales
limones |

Negatives

Just put *no* in front of the phrase:

no hay patatas   no me gusta

Exercises

1   You're at the *estanco.* Fill in your part of the conversation from the following list:

seis sellos de diez pesetas/¿cuánto es?/buenos días/¿hay postales?/cinco, por favor/no, gracias

Empleado	Buenos días. ¿Qué desea?
Usted	(*greet him; you want postcards*)...............
	....
Empleado	Sí, cierto. ¿Cuántas quiere?
Usted	(*you want five*) ....
Empleado	¿Algo más?
Usted	(*you want six ten-peseta stamps*)..............
	....
Empleado	¿Algo más?
Usted	(*no, thank you; you want to know the cost*) ....
Empleado	Ochenta y cinco pesetas, por favor.

How much were you charged? Work it out from the list of numbers on page 63. ....

2 You've tried grilled sardines and want to buy some more. Fill in this dialogue with the fishmonger.

Pescadero	Buenos días. ¿Qué quiere?
Usted	(*greet him; you want sardines*) ....
	....
Pescadero	Sí. ¿Cuánto quiere?
Usted	(*you want enough for eight people*).........
	....
Pescadero	¿Vale?
Usted	(*you don't think that is quite enough*)......
	....
Pescadero	¿Vale?
Usted	(*yes, that's right*) ....
Pescadero	¿Quiere algo más?
Usted	(*that's all; you want to pay*) ....
	....
Pescadero	Ciento veinticinco pesetas en total.

What was the total?...

3

a   Are these sums correct? Correct them if not.

dos + cuatro = seis   ....

seis + tres   = ocho   ....

dos + ocho   = siete   ....

cinco + dos = diez   ....

ocho − uno   = nueve   ....

diez − cuatro = cinco   ....

b   You're being offered alternatives of size and price
by the shopkeeper. Use the information he gives you
to guess which is which. Tick the correct word
alongside each.

¿Quiere un pan <u>pequeño,</u> de medio kilo?	large/small
¿O prefiere un pan <u>grande</u> de un kilo?	large/small
¿Quiere un melón <u>grande</u> de tres kilos?	large/small
¿O prefiere un melón <u>pequeño</u> de dos kilos?	large/small
¿Quiere manzanas <u>caras</u> a diez pesetas el medio kilo?	cheap/dear
¿O prefiere manzanas <u>baratas</u> a ocho pesetas el medio?	cheap/dear
¿Quiere postales <u>caras</u> de cinco pesetas cada una?	cheap/dear
¿O prefiere postales <u>baratas</u> de tres pesetas cada una?	cheap/dear

If someone says *muy caro* when they're offered
something, what do they mean? ....
And if they say *muy barato*? ....

....

4* You're shopping at the grocer's. Fill in the dialogue with the shopkeeper (*el tendero*).

Tendero	Buenas tardes. ¿En qué le puedo servir?
Usted	(*greet him and ask for wine*) ....
	....
Tendero	¿Vino? Sí, a cien pesetas el litro. ¿Cuánto quiere?
Usted	(*ask for a litre*) ....
	....
Tendero	Muy bien. ¿Necesita algo más?
Usted	(*you want some coffee*) ....
Tendero	Sí. ¿Cuánto quiere – un kilo, medio kilo?
Usted	(*find out how much it is*) ....
	....
Tendero	Seiscientas pesetas el kilo.
Usted	(*you'll have half a kilo*) ....
	....
Tendero	De acuerdo. ¿Alguna cosa más?
Usted	(*you want a loaf of bread*) ....
Tendero	¿Eso es todo?
Usted	(*Yes, thanks*) ....
Tendero	Cuatrocientas diez pesetas en total.

How much is the bill? (*Write it down in figures*) ....

*Check your answers to this exercise at the beginning of Programme 3.

Worth knowing

Being served

There are many ways of being asked

what do you want?	and	*anything else?*
¿qué quiere (usted)?		¿algo más?
¿qué desea (usted)?		¿quiere algo más?
¿qué deseaba?		¿necesita algo más?
¿querría?		¿alguna cosa más?
¿en qué le puedo servir?		¿eso es todo?

and of being told how much things cost:

son exactamente ochocientas pesetas
that's exactly 800 pesetas
nueve pesetas en total *nine pesetas altogether*
cada sello es/vale/cuesta diez pesetas
each stamp is/is worth/costs ten pesetas

Shopping for food

Most food that we're used to in England is available
in Spanish markets and supermarkets. Dairy products
are generally expensive, but some fruit and vegetables
are very cheap. Alcoholic drinks are sold at all grocers.
Bread is bought at *la panadería* (the baker's).

Postcards, stamps and postal service

Postcards and stamps are sold at tobacconists
(*estancos*) and kiosks which are easily recognisable
by their red and yellow signs.

Postboxes are yellow with a red post office symbol.
Correos is the Post Office and provides the usual
services. Letters for Poste Restante should be sent to
the addressee, *lista de Correos*, followed by the name
of the town or city.

Telephones

For trunk calls you should look for a *Teléfono
interurbano/internacional* with a green band at the
top, or go to the central exchange, *La Telefónica.*
Local and long distance calls are automatic and
timed. Arm yourself with plenty of 5, 25 and 50
peseta pieces!

For a call to the UK, dial 07 and wait for a high-
pitched dialling tone, then dial 44 for Great Britain,
followed by the town code (without the first 0) and
the number. For example, for London number, 01-
246 8047,.you would dial 07 . . . 44 1 246 8047.

The chemist's

The chemist's, *la farmacia*, has a sign with a green cross. There you can get anything from aspirins (*aspirinas*) to medicines that may require a prescription in England. If the *farmacia* you go to is closed there'll be a list displayed of the nearest chemists which are open (*de guardia* or *de turno*).

Garages

For oil and petrol go to the *estación de servicio* or *gasolinera*. Petrol grades are as follows: *normal* – 85 octane; *super* – 96 octane; *extra* – 98 octane. Multigrade oil is *aceite multigrado.* For repairs you'll need *un taller*, a repair shop – the entrance is marked by red and white stripes.

Tobacco and cigarettes

Tabaco rubio is Virginia or blond tobacco, but *tabaco negro,* dark tobacco, is usually smoked in Spain. Spanish brands are cheaper than imported ones.

Currency

The Spanish unit of currency is the *peseta*. The smallest coin is a 10-céntimo piece (one-tenth of a peseta). There are also coins worth 50 céntimos, and 1, 5, 25, 50 and 100 pesetas. The 5-peseta coin is commonly called *un duro.* There are notes of 100, 500 and 1000 pesetas.

Where to buy what you need

un supermercado (supermarket)
una frutería (fruit shop)
una tienda de ultramarinos ⎤
una tienda de comestibles ⎦ (grocer's)
una pescadería (fishmonger)
una carnicería (butcher)

3 Getting around

Conversations

Do you speak English?

Turista   ¿Habla inglés?
Señor   No, señora, lo siento. ¿Habla español?
Turista   Sí, un poco.

Asking directions

En el café

Turista   Por favor, ¿hay lavabos?
Camarero ¿Cómo?
Turista   ¿Hay lavabos?
Camarero Ah, lavabos. Sí, señora. En el patio.
Turista   En el patio, gracias.
Camarero De nada.

En la calle

Señor   Oiga, por favor, ¿una farmacia?
Señora ¿Una farmacia? Mmm, en la Plaza Mayor.
Señor   En la Plaza Mayor. ¿Dónde está?
Señora Al final de esta calle.

Señora Por favor, ¿hay un banco por aquí?
Señor   ¿Un banco? Sí. En la Calle de Valladolid.
Señora En la Calle de Valladolid. ¿Dónde está?
Señor   ¿Dónde está? Pues, al lado de la catedral.
por aquí   *round here*

Turista Oiga, por favor. ¿Hay un camping por aquí?
Señor   ¿Un camping? Pues, el Camping Quijote. Al
          lado del río.
Turista Al lado del río. El río, ¿dónde está?
Señor   Por la carretera de Vigo.
por la carretera de Vigo   *along the main road to Vigo*

Señora	¿Hay pan?
Señor	Aquí, no. Al lado.
Señora	Al lado. Gracias.
Señor	De nada.

Señor	Por favor, ¿dónde hay un buzón?
Señora	¿Un buzón? Pues, al otro lado de la calle.
Señor	Al otro lado. Muchas gracias.

Señora	¿Me puede decir dónde hay una tienda de recuerdos?
Señor	Sí, con mucho gusto. Puede usted ir siguiendo la calle y a unos cien metros va a encontrar una zapatería. Da la vuelta a la esquina y justo entonces la encontrará.
Señora	O sea, ¿está al lado de la zapatería?
Señor	No, está al otro lado de la calle.
Señora	Al otro lado de la calle.
Señor	Sí, señora.
Señora	Muy bien, muchas gracias.
Señor	De nada.

¿me puede decir . . . ?   *can you tell me . . . ?*
con mucho gusto   *it's a pleasure*
puede usted ir siguiendo la calle   *you can keep following this street*
va a encontrar una zapatería   *you'll come across a shoe shop*
da la vuelta a la esquina   *you go round the corner*
y justo entonces la encontrará   *and you'll find it just there*
o sea   *in other words*

Beginning of side one, cassette two

Turista	Oiga, por favor, ¿la oficina de turismo?
Señora	¿La oficina de turismo? Está aquí mismo, al final de la Calle de Valladolid.
Turista	¿Cómo?
Señora	Aquí mismo, al final de la Calle de Valladolid.
Turista	Más despacio, más despacio, por favor.
Señora	Al final de la Calle de Valladolid.

Turista	Por favor, más despacio.
Señora	Calle de Valladolid. Al final.
Turista	Ah, Calle de Valladolid, al final. Gracias.
Señora	De nada, Adiós
Turista	Adiós

aquí mismo   *right here*

Señor	La Avenida de Cataluña, ¿está lejos?
Señora	No, no está lejos, está muy cerca, al final de la calle, a la derecha.

Turista	Por favor, ¿hay una estación de servicio por aquí?
Señor	Sí, hay una en la Calle del Rey.
Turista	La Calle del Rey. ¿Está lejos?
Señor	No, no está lejos. Está aquí cerca.

aquí cerca   *near here*

Turista	Por favor, la catedral, ¿está lejos?
Señora	¿La catedral? Sí, está un poco lejos – a medio kilómetro, más o menos.

Turista	Por favor, ¿el Restaurante Granada?
Señora	¿El Restaurante Granada? Sí, en esta misma calle, a la izquierda.

en esta misma calle   *in this street*

Finding your way by car

Señora	Oiga, por favor, ¿para Sevilla?
Señor	Por ahí, a la derecha.
Señora	Más despacio, por favor.
Señor	A la derecha.

Señora	Oiga, por favor, ¿para Barcelona?
Señor	Pues, todo seguido, recto, recto.

Señora	Por favor, ¿dónde está la Plaza Mayor?
Señor	Cuando llegue a los semáforos, tuerza usted a la izquierda. Después, siga recto hasta la primera calle y luego tuerce a la derecha, y allí está la Plaza Mayor.
Señora	Gracias.
Señor	De nada. Adiós, con mucho gusto.
Señora	Adiós

Cuando llegue a los semáforos . . . *when you get to the traffic lights . . .*
tuerza usted *turn*
después . . . y luego *then . . . and then*
tuerce *you turn*
siga recto hasta la primera calle *keep straight on until the first street*

Language summary

Asking the way

Can you tell me the way to . . . ?

(oiga) por favor,	¿un banco? ¿el lavabo? ¿un buzón?

in the . . .

en	la Calle de Valladolid el patio la Avenida de Cataluña

Where is there a . . . ?

¿dónde hay	un restaurante? una farmacia? un café?

at the end of . . .

al final de	esta calle la avenida

Where is the . . . ?

¿dónde está	la Avenida de Cataluña? la Plaza Mayor? la Calle de Valladolid?

beside . . .

al lado	del río de la catedral

here/over there

aquí
ahí, allí

the first on the right/left

la primera a la
derecha/izquierda

left/right/straight on

a la izquierda L↑
a la derecha R↑
todo seguido/recto

Is it far?

¿Está lejos?

it's far away/(very) close

sí, está lejos
no, está (muy) cerca

. . . minutes/metres away

a unos diez minutos
a unos cien metros

Understanding what people say

Do you speak . . . ?

¿habla (usted) inglés?
español?

yes, a little/no, I'm sorry

sí, un poco
no, lo siento

What did you say?

¿cómo?

slower, please

más despacio, por favor

Explanations

por

por | aquí HERE | round here, this way
| ahí THERE | along there, that way
| la carretera de Vigo | along the main road to Vigo

hasta . . . luego

hasta (until) and *luego* (then) which you've met as
hasta luego (see p13) are also used separately:

recto hasta la primera calle *straight on until the first street*
luego a la derecha *then to the right*

Exercises

1 What questions did you ask to get the following replies? e.g. for (a) you must have asked: *La catedral, ¿está lejos?*

a ...*LA CATEDRAL ¿ESTÁ IEJOS*...

No, la catedral está muy cerca.   *NEAR BY*

b *DÓNDE ESTÁ LA AVENIDA D CATAUNA*

La Avenida de Cataluña está aquí a la izquierda. *LT*

c *POR FAVOR IA PLAZA DE TOROS ESTA IZJOS*

Sí, la plaza de toros *(the bull-ring)* está un poco lejos.

d ...*POR FAVOR ¿UN BANCO CENTRAL?*...

El Banco Central está en la Calle de Valladolid, a la izquierda.

e *EL CAMPING QUIJOTE ¿ESTÁ IEJOS?*

¿El Camping Quijote? No, está aquí cerca. *RT HERE*

f *DONDE ESTA LE ESTACION SERVICIO*

La estación de servicio está aquí a la derecha. *RT*

g *DÓNDE HAY EL TALLER POR FAVOR*

El taller está por ahí, a la derecha. *RT*

CORRECTIONS.

2 Whoever gave you the above information must be quite a stranger to *Mongoya* – the answers are only sometimes right! Check them from the map on page 31 – you're both in the *Plaza Mayor*, facing away from the river, up the *Calle de Valladolid*. What should his answers have been?

a ✓ ESTA MUY CERCA
b RT ESTA LA DERECHA
c CLOSE BY ESTA MUY CERCA
d RT ESTA LA DERECHA
e FAR AWAY. NO, ESTA LEJOS
f LT ESTA AQUI LA IZQUIERDA
g LT A LA IZQUIERDA

3 You're finding your way around *Mongoya*. First ask the appropriate questions, then fill in the answers from the list below, following the directions on the map.

en/al final/al lado/al otro lado/al final

a You're outside the *Hotel España* and you need a postbox to post some cards home.

Usted Por favor, UN BUZÓN

Señor Aquí A LA IZQUIERDA

b Back at the hotel, you ask the receptionist where the *Plaza Mayor* is as you've arranged to meet a friend there.

Usted Por favor, DÓNDE ESTA PLAZA MAYOR

Recepcionista Está AL DERECHA de esta Avenida.

c Next you want to know where the Tourist Office is.

Usted ¿Dónde está OFICINA DE TURISMO

Recepcionista Está LA DERECHA de la Calle de Valladolid.

d   You'd like a drink before starting your sightseeing. Ask the man in the tourist office for a café.

Usted   Por favor, ¿DONDE HAY? UN CAFÉ.

Señor   Ahí, ...Al FINAL..... de la calle.

e   You remember that you have to buy some sun tan lotion. Ask the waiter in the café where the chemist's is.

Usted   Por favor, DONDE HAY UNA FARMACIA

Camarero   Está A LA IZQUIERDA la Plaza Mayor.

4*   Your car has broken down in the Plaza Mayor, just in front of the cathedral. Your need a repair shop (*un taller*). Fill in your part of the conversation with a passer-by.

Usted   *(you want to know if he speaks English)* ....
POR FAVOR HABLA (USTED) INGLÉS?

Señor   No, lo siento, no hablo inglés.

Usted   *(you'll have to ask him in Spanish for a repair shop)* POR FAVOR
DONDE HAY UN TALLER?

Señor   ¿Un taller? Hay uno en la Calle Pérez Galdos.

Usted   *(you want to know if that's far away)* ....
GRACIAS ESTA LEJOS?

Señor   Está un poco lejos. A unos diez minutos.

Usted   *(ask him where it is)* ....¿DONDE ESTA?

Señor   Al final de la calle, la primera a la derecha.
Luego todo seguido – la primera a la izquierda es la Calle Pérez Galdos.

Usted   *(he's going too fast; ask him to slow down)* ...
MAS DESPACIO, POR FAVOR

Señor   Al final de esta calle.

Usted   *(you repeat the basic information each time, and follow it on your map)* ....

Señor   La primera a la derecha.

*Don't forget to check your answers at the beginning of the next programme.

Usted	....
Señor	Luego todo seguido.
Usted	....
Señor	Luego la primera a la izquierda.
Usted	....
Señor	El taller está a la derecha de la calle.
Usted	....
	(thank him) ....
Señor	De nada. Adiós.

Worth knowing

Finding your way around

If you ask a stranger the way and it isn't very far he may offer to walk with you:

yo le enseño I'll show you
yo le acompaño I'll go along with you.

In Spanish towns the local tourist office (*la oficina de turismo*) will provide you with general information, plans, guides, brochures and lists of accommodation and restaurants. Street names are well marked, but Spaniards often refer to the main street in a city as *la Gran Vía*, even though its official name is different. There's a *Plaza Mayor* in every town where people meet for a drink or a chat.

Signs

You'll need to recognise these:

TOILETS	*Lavabos*	LADIES	*Señoras*
	Servicios		*Damas*
	Retrete	GENTS	*Caballeros*
			Hombres
WAY IN	*Entrada*	PUSH	*Empujar*
WAY OUT	*Salida*	PULL	*Tirar*

Roads

In Spain pedestrian crossings are very similar to our panda crossings. The instructions read:

ESPEREN	Wait
PEATONES	Pedestrians
PASEN	Cross

Traffic police are very strict about pedestrian crossing rules.

The motoring organisations or the Spanish Tourist Office in London will provide information about traffic signs and regulations.

Roads are designated by letters and numbers:

A roads are motorways
N roads are main roads
C roads are minor roads

Toll roads – the word PEAJE on a sign on a motorway, etc., means you have to pay a toll.

Spain conforms to the International Highway Code – there is priority for vehicles coming from the right and rigorous application of no-overtaking restrictions.

Police

Spanish police are empowered to fine you on the spot for traffic infringements (*una multa* is the word for a fine). The Civil Guard (*la Guardia Civil*) can be recognised by their patent leather hats and green uniforms, and the municipal police wear blue. Police on traffic control duty use whistles. They wear grey uniforms with white helmets and white gloves. Most Spanish policemen are armed.

4 Getting the time

Conversations

Asking whether and when you can do things

En el taller

Señorita	No funciona el coche. ¿Se puede mirar el motor, por favor?
Empleado	Sí, se puede, señorita.

En la calle

Señor	¿Se puede aparcar?
Señora	¿Cómo?
Señor	¿Se puede aparcar?
Señora	No. Aquí no se puede. Está prohibido.

En el tren

Señor	¿Se puede fumar?
Camarera	No, aquí no se puede. Está prohibido fumar.

En el restaurante

Señorita	¿Se puede cenar?
Camarero	¿Cenar? Ahora no se puede.
Señorita	¿Cuándo?
Camarero	A las nueve.
Señora	¿Cuándo se puede cenar?
Camarero	A las diez.
Señora	¿Se puede cenar?
Camarero	Se puede cenar a las nueve y cuarto.
Señora	¿Se puede desayunar?
Camarero	Se puede desayunar a las ocho y media.

Señora	¿Se puede comer?
Camarero	Se puede comer a las tres menos cuarto.
Señora	¿Se puede comer?
Camarero	Sí, se puede.
Señora	¿Hasta cuándo?
Camarero	Pues, hasta las cuatro.
Señora	¿Se puede cenar?
Camarero	Sí, se puede cenar desde las nueve hasta las once y media.

Asking whether places are open or closed

En la calle

Señorita	Por favor, ¿una farmacia?
Señor	Sí, señorita, al final de la calle.
Señorita	¿Está abierta?
Señor	Sí, sí, señorita.
Señorita	Por favor, la farmacia, ¿está abierta?
Señor	No, está cerrada.
Señorita	¿Hasta cuándo?
Señor	Hasta mañana.
Señora	Por favor, ¿hay un estanco abierto?
Señor	¿Un estanco abierto? No, señora, todo está cerrado. Hoy es fiesta.

hoy es fiesta   *today is a holiday*

En la estación de servicio

Empleado	Buenas tardes.
Señorita	Buenas tardes.
Empleado	¿Quiere gasolina?
Señorita	No, gracias. No funciona el motor. ¿Se puede reparar?
Empleado	No, señorita, lo siento. El taller está cerrado.

Señorita   ¿<u>Cerrado</u>?
Empleado   Sí, señorita. Está cerrado por la tarde.

por la tarde   *in the afternoon*

Beginning of side two, cassette two

En la calle

Señora   <u>Por favor, ¿la oficina de turismo?</u>
Señor   La oficina de turismo está cerrada.
Señora   <u>¿Hasta cuándo?</u>
Señor   Hasta mañana por la mañana.

mañana por la mañana   *tomorrow morning*

Enquiring about train times

En la oficina de la RENFE (Spanish railways)

Señora   <u>Valencia, por favor.</u>
Empleado   Valencia, muy bien. ¿Quiere viajar esta tarde o mañana por la mañana?
Señora   <u>Por la mañana, por favor.</u>
Empleado   Hay un tren a las nueve treinta y cinco.
Señora   <u>¿Cuándo?</u>
Empleado   A las nueve treinta y cinco.
Señora   <u>¿Cuándo llega a Valencia?</u>
Empleado   Llega a las dieciséis veinte.
Señora   <u>¿Cuándo?</u>
Empleado   A las dieciséis veinte.
Señora   <u>Vale, gracias.</u>

¿Quiere viajar . . . ?   *Do you want to travel . . . ?*

Language summary

How to say 'It doesn't work'

the car	el coche	
the phone	el teléfono	
the lift	el ascensor	no funciona
the engine	el motor	
the toilet	el lavabo	

Asking what you can do
Is it possible to . . . ?

¿se puede	desayunar? *have breakfast* comer? *have lunch/eat* cenar? *have dinner* reparar? *repair* cambiar? *change* aparcar? *park* reservar? *reserve* beber? *drink* abrir? *open* cerrar? *close* comprar? *buy*	

yes, it is
sí, se puede

no, it isn't
no, no se puede

you're not allowed to . .

está prohibido	aparcar *park* fumar *smoke* tocar *touch*

Finding out when things happen
When?

¿cuándo?

now/then/after
ahora/luego/después

today/tomorrow
hoy/mañana

*in the morning/
afternoon or evening/
at night*

por	la mañana la tarde la noche

When is it possible to . ?

¿cuándo se puede	desayunar? comer? cenar?

at . . . o'clock etc.
a la una

a las	dos tres *etc.*

from . . .

desde las	siete dos

to . . .

hasta las	ocho seis

**When does the . . .
arrive/leave?**

¿cuándo │ llega │ el tren?
         │ sale │ el tele-
         │   │ grama?
         │   │ el auto-
         │   │ bús?

at half past . . .

a las │ cuatro │ y media
      │ cinco │

at quarter past . . .

a las │ siete │ y cuarto
      │ ocho │

at quarter to . . .

a las │ siete │ menos
      │ nueve │ cuarto

**When is there a . . .
for . . . ?**

¿cuándo hay │ un tren
            │ un coche

para │ Valencia?
     │ Madrid?

at . . . minutes past . . .

a las │ diez │ y cinco
      │ seis │ y diez
      │   │ y veinte

at . . . minutes to . . .

a las │ tres │ menos cinco
      │ ocho │ menos diez
      │   │ menos veinte

Is it open?

¿está abierto(a)?

**yes, it's open/no, it's
closed**

sí, está abierto(a)

no, │ no está abierto(a)
    │ está cerrado(a)

Until when?

¿hasta cuándo?

**until tomorrow/
2 o'clock etc.**

hasta │ mañana
      │ las dos *etc.*

Explanations

no funciona

This goes either before or after the name of the thing that's not working, depending on which you wish to emphasise – or which you think of first: *no funciona el coche* and *el coche no funciona* are equally correct.

¿se puede?

This literally means 'can one?', 'is it possible?'. Since verbs are always given in dictionaries in the infinitive form (e.g. *fumar* – to smoke; *comer* – to eat), you can slot in any verb you need (e.g. *¿se puede fumar?*; *¿se puede comer?*). *¿Se puede?* can be used by itself: you may want to get past people into a shop – simply ask *¿Se puede?* and the reply may be *Sí, sí, pase usted* (yes, go through) or you may need an extra chair in a café: ask *¿Se puede?* and you may be told *Sí, sí, llévesela* (yes, take it).

desayunar . . . comer . . . cenar

These mean 'to have breakfast', 'to have lunch', 'to have dinner'. The names of the meals are *el desayuno, la comida, la cena.*

a las doce

People often use *a mediodía* (at midday) and *a medianoche* (at midnight).

Exercises

1   The notice outside the office says:

JORNADA INTENSIVA †
ABIERTO 8.00–1.30
CERRADO POR LA TARDE

but you've been given a lot of conflicting information about its opening times. Correct the following statements where necessary.

†   jornada intensiva   *intensive working day*

a La oficina está cerrada a las tres menos cuarto........
   CORRECT

b Está cerrada por la mañana. ..... *ESTA ABIERTA*

c La oficina está abierta a las nueve y media... *CORRECT*

d La oficina está cerrada a las cuatro menos cuarto..
   CORRECT

e Está abierta por la noche. ..... *CERRADO*

f Está abierta desde las nueve hasta la una y cuarto..
   ..... *LAS OCHO – LAS UNA MEDIA*

2 These are the mealtimes at the *Hotel España*. What answers would you get to the following questions?

a ¿Cuándo se puede comer?   *LUNCH*
   ..... *A LA UNA*

b ¿Hasta cuándo?
   ..... *LAS TRES Y MEDIA*

c ¿Cuándo se puede desayunar?   *BREAKFAST*
   LAS SIETE Y MEDIA

d ¿Hasta cuándo?
   A LAS DIEZ MEDIA

e ¿Hasta cuándo se puede cenar?
   LAS OCHO Y MEDIA

f ¿Se puede cenar a las diez? ..... *SI SE PUEDE*

g ¿Se puede desayunar a las seis y media?
   ..... *NO SE PUEDE*

h ¿Se puede comer a las doce? *NO SE PUEDE*

Desayuno — hasta

Comida — hasta

Cena — hasta

3

a   You're at the RENFE office (Spanish railways) and the official gives you this information:

'Sí, hay un tren para Barcelona a las dieciséis cuarenta. Llega a las veintitrés veinte.'

Where do you want to go? _BARCELONA_

When should you be at the station to catch the train? (12-hour clock time) _4:40_   _11-20_

When would you arrive at your destination? (12-hour clock time) _11-20_

b   For a shorter journey, you decide to use the bus service. This is what the travel agent tells you:

'No hay autobús para Sevilla hasta esta tarde, a las diecinueve cincuenta. Llega a Sevilla a las veintiún horas.'

Is there a bus in the morning? ....

When should you tell your Seville friends to meet you? (12-hour clock time) ....

When should you catch the bus? (12-hour clock time) ....

4* You want to book a train seat to Valencia. First you find out at your hotel if the RENFE office is open. Fill in the dialogue.

Usted	*(ask if the RENFE is open)* ....
	....
Recepcionista	¿La RENFE? Sí, está abierta.
Usted	*(you find out how long it stays open)*
	....
Recepcionista	Hasta las cuatro de la tarde, me parece. Sí, hasta las cuatro.

Usted	(you repeat the time and say thank you) ....
Recepcionista	De nada.

So you go along to the RENFE office.

Usted	(you want to go to Valencia)......................... ....
Empleado	Muy bien. ¿Cuándo quiere viajar, esta tarde o mañana?
Usted	(you want to go tomorrow).........................
Empleado	¿Por la mañana o por la tarde?
Usted	(you want to go in the morning)................ ....
Empleado	Hay un tren que sale a las 9.35.
Usted	(you repeat the time in words) .... (you also want to know when it arrives)... ....
Empleado	Llega a las 16.20.
Usted	(you didn't catch what he said) ....
Empleado	A las dieciséis veinte, o sea a las 4.20 de la tarde.
Usted	(repeat the time in words) .... (tell him that's OK, and thank him)............ ....

Worth knowing

Opening times

Meals – Spaniards tend to have lunch and dinner later than we do in England. Restaurants stay open for lunch until quite late in the afternoon and serve dinner from around 8.30 p.m. until after midnight.

Banks are open only in the mornings.

Shops stay open later than in this country, with a break for *siesta*, usually around 1.00–4.30 p.m.

Watch out for *fiestas* when all the shops are closed – an information bulletin will be available from the local *oficina de turismo.*

In the summer, businesses and offices often switch to a *jornada intensiva*, an intensive working day, usually from 8.00 a.m. to 1.30 p.m.

Cinemas and theatres – matinées on Sundays and holidays at 4.30 p.m.; otherwise at 7.00 p.m., with an evening performance at 10.00–11.00 p.m. Theatres are usually closed on Mondays.

Museums (*museos*) open morning and late afternoon.

Bullfights and football matches take place regularly on Sundays, starting late in the afternoon.

Booking in advance – tickets (*entradas*) for cinemas, theatres, concerts, etc., can be obtained in advance from the box office (*la taquilla*). Cafés and bars often supply tickets in advance for bullfights and football matches.

Prohibitive notices

PROHIBIDO FUMAR	No smoking
PROHIBIDO ESCUPIR	No spitting
ESTACIONAMIENTO PROHIBIDO	No parking
PROHIBIDO EL PASO	No entry
PROHIBIDO PISAR EL CÉSPED	Don't walk on the grass
PELIGRO	Danger

In the centre of towns, *la zona azul* is the blue zone in which parking is restricted. In cities, illegally parked cars may be towed away by *la grúa* (the crane), and can only be recovered on payment of a fine.

Travel information

Information leaflets on Spain have been prepared by the Spanish National Tourist Office, 57 St. James's Street, London SW1.

RENFE *(Red Nacional de Ferrocarriles Españoles)* is the Spanish railway company.

Trains – the *Talgo* and the *TER* are luxury expresses; *expresos* and *automotores* are slower; *semidirectos* and *omnibuses* or *ferrobuses* are local trains.

Prices are reckoned on a kilometric basis and according to class (first or second – the third class is rarely found these days). Return tickets (*un billete de ida y vuelta*) or single only (*ida sólo*) can be bought. Books of coupons (*billetes kilométricos*) are available to individuals or groups and they entitle you to 3,000 or 12,000 kilometres of cheap travel over a period. Supplements have to be paid on the *Talgo* and *TER* and it's worth booking your tickets in advance from the local RENFE office, as trains are crowded and booking offices are often closed before departure. Porters (*mozos*) wear blue smocks and caps.

Planes – Iberia Airlines, 169 Regent Street, London W1, have details of domestic services.

Buses and coaches – coaches are run by private companies. You can get details from a local travel agency (*agencia de viajes*). They are usually a cheap way of travelling.

Taxis – fares by meter, similar to England. The sign LIBRE and a green light at night indicate that the taxi is available for hire. You can hire *gran turismo* taxis for long journeys.

Metro – the underground railway. There are systems in Madrid and Barcelona.

Hitchhiking – legal, although the authorities do not encourage it.

5 Getting to your destination

There are not many new structures in this programme. Its main purpose is to show you how to apply what you've already learned to other situations.

Conversations

Today is your first full day alone in Spain. On arrival in the country you clear Customs, catch a bus to the town centre, then take a taxi to your hotel. At your hotel you check in (or, if you haven't booked in advance, you find a room), after which you go off to meet some new friends. Finally you all go to the restaurant where you have booked a table and have ordered a large paella.

Clearing customs

En la aduana

Señor	Buenos días.
Aduanero	Buenos días, señores.
Señora	Buenos días.
Aduanero	Pasaporte, por favor.
Señor	Sí, un momento. Tome.
Aduanero	¿Dónde tienen ustedes sus maletas?
Señor	Un momento. *(he goes and gets them)*
Aduanero	¿Haría usted el favor de abrirla? *(he examines one of their suitcases)*
Señora	Muchas gracias.
Aduanero	Adiós.
Señor y Señora	Adiós.
Aduanero	Que tengan una buena estancia en España.
Señor	Muchas gracias. Adiós.

tome *here you are*
¿dónde tienen ustedes sus maletas? *where are your suitcases?*

¿haría usted el favor de abrirla? *would you please open it? (very formal)*

que tengan una buena estancia en España *have a good stay in Spain*

Getting transport

En la calle

Turista	<u>Por favor, ¿el autobús?</u>
Señor	¿Para el centro?
Turista	<u>Sí, por favor.</u>
Señor	La parada está aquí, a la izquierda.

Turista	<u>¡Taxi! ¡Taxi!</u> *(taxi stops)* <u>Hotel España, por favor. ¿Está lejos?</u>
Taxista	No, no está lejos. Está cerca, muy cerca. *(taxi arrives at hotel)*
Turista	<u>¿Cuánto es?</u>
Taxista	Son treinta pesetas, y con las maletas, cincuenta. Cincuenta pesetas en total.
Turista	<u>¿Cómo?</u>
Taxista	Treinta pesetas, por favor, y con las maletas, cincuenta.
Turista	<u>Gracias.</u>

la parada *bus stop*

con las maletas *with the suitcases* (there is often a separate charge)

Checking in

En el hotel

Recepcionista	¿Su nombre, por favor?
María Antonia	Marcos. Señora María Antonia Marcos.
Recepcionista	Un momento, vamos a ver. Sí, sí, aquí está. La habitación número ciento treinta y cinco.
María Antonia	<u>¿Cómo?</u>
Recepcionista	La habitación número ciento treinta y cinco.
María Antonia	<u>Más despacio, por favor.</u>

Recepcionista	Ciento treinta y cinco – uno, tres, cinco.
María Antonia	Gracias.
Recepcionista	De nada.

vamos a ver   *let's see*

Booking a room

Turista	¿Hay habitaciones, por favor?
Recepcionista	Sí, señor. ¿Para cuántas personas?
Turista	Para dos.
Recepcionista	¿Para dos? ¿Con dos camas o con cama de matrimonio?
Turista	¿Cómo?
Recepcionista	¿Con dos camas o con cama de matrimonio?
Turista	Con cama de matrimonio, por favor.
Recepcionista	¿Para cuántas noches?
Turista	Dos.
Recepcionista	Dos noches, muy bien. Tiene la habitación número noventa y ocho.
Turista	¿Cómo?
Recepcionista	Noventa y ocho – nueve, ocho.
Turista	Noventa y ocho.
Recepcionista	Sí, señor.
Turista	Gracias.
Recepcionista	De nada.

Recepcionista	Su pasaporte, por favor, *(taking down details)* Número de pasaporte – uno, tres, cinco, siete, nueve, seis. ¿Su nombre?
Turista	Marcos.
Recepcionista	Ah, sí, Marcos.

Getting to know people

Eduardo	¿Cómo se llama?
María Antonia	María Antonia. ¿Cómo se llama?

Eduardo	Eduardo.
María Antonia	¿Es inglés?
Eduardo	No. ¿Es inglesa?
María Antonia	Sí.
Eduardo	¿De dónde?
María Antonia	De Londres.

Señora	Aquí le presento al Señor López.
Señor	Encantado.
Sr López	¿Qué tal está?
Señor	¿Cómo está usted?
Sr López	Muy bien, gracias.
Señora	¿Quieren ustedes que vayamos a algún sitio a tomar algo y hablamos?
Señor	Sí, me gustaría tomar un café.
Señora	Bien. ¿Y usted?
Sr López	Yo prefiero un té.
Señor	¿Vamos?
Señora	Sí, vámonos.
Sr López	De acuerdo.

¿quieren ustedes que vayamos a algún sitio a tomar algo y hablamos? *shall we go somewhere for a drink and a chat?*
me gustaría tomar un café *I'd like a coffee*
¿vamos? *shall we go?*
sí, vámonos *yes, let's go*
de acuerdo *yes, of course*

Dining out

En el restaurante

Eduardo	Oiga, por favor.
Camarera	Sí, señores, ¿qué desean?
Eduardo	Una paella para ocho personas. Está pedida. El nombre es Delgado.
Camarera	Ah, sí, la paella para ustedes. Muy bien, un momento. . . . ¿Y qué quieren beber con la paella? ¿Vino? ¿Cerveza?
Eduardo	Vino, por favor. Vino blanco.

está pedida *it's been ordered*
¿qué quieren beber? *what do you want to drink?*

Language summary

Being asked your name . . .
Officially . . .

¿su nombre, por favor?	Eduardo Delgado María Antonia Marcos
¿su apellido?	Delgado Marcos

Less formally

¿cómo se llama?	Carlos Juanita

and where you're from
Nationality

¿es | inglés?
americano? *(man)* | sí

 | inglesa?
americana? *(woman)* | no, | español *(man)*
española *(woman)*

Which town?

¿de dónde? | de | Manchester
Londres
Dublin
Cardiff
Aberdeen

Being introduced

le
presento | a María
a Juanita
al Señor López | encantado *(man)*
encantada *(woman)*

or simply | María
Pepe
Eduardo | mucho gusto

encantado . . . encantada

You use this not only when you're introduced to someone but also when you're saying *adiós* to somebody you've just been introduced to:
'Encantado, adiós.'

¿Cómo se llama?

This is used to ask someone's name. It is also used to ask the name of things and places – so you can use it to learn new words.

Exercises

Exercises 1 and 2 refer directly to programme 5. The others revise what you have learned in other programmes. There are reference numbers to help you check back.

1 Wherever you stay in Spain, you will have to fill in a registration form, *una ficha. La ficha* requires you to fill in the following information:

Apellido **BORROW**	Nombre **GEORGE**
Fecha de nacimiento **6.12.38**	Nacionalidad **INGLÉS**
Lugar de nacimiento **NEWCASTLE**	Dirección **8 THE LANE**
	LONDON SE2
Nº. de pasaporte **79368A72**	exp. en **LONDRES**
	el **15.8.77**
Firma del viajero: **G Borrow**	

a From the details you find filled in, what do you guess all the spaces refer to? Fill in the English words in the brackets in the form below.

b Fill in your own particulars.

Apellido	Nombre
( )	( )
Fecha de Nacimiento	Nacionalidad
( )	( )
Lugar de nacimiento	Dirección
( )	( )
N⁰. de Pasaporte	exp. en
( )	( )
	el
	( )

Firma del viajero:
( )

c Now you're talking to someone you've met.
Answer his questions and ask your own.

Señor español	Buenas tardes.
Usted	....
Señor español	¿Es americano?
Usted	*(no, you're English)* ....
	....
Señor español	Ah, sí. ¿De dónde?
Usted	*(tell him)* ....
Señor español	¿Cómo se llama?
Usted	*(tell him)* ....
	(you want to know his name) ....
	....
Señor español	Juan Alonso.
Usted	*(say you're pleased to meet him)* ....
	....

2 You're a couple with two children, and you want to reserve two rooms, one for yourselves and one for your children. You need two double rooms, one with double bed and one with twin beds, for three nights.

a   Fill in your part in the conversation.

Recepcionista	Buenas tardes, señores.
Usted	*(greet her and ask if there are any rooms available)* ....
Recepcionista	Sí, hay varias. ¿Cuántas habitaciones quieren?
Usted	....
Recepcionista	¿Para cuántas personas?
Usted	....
Recepcionista	¿Dos habitaciones para dos personas cada una?
Usted	*(if you think that's correct, say so)* ....
Recepcionista	¿Para cuántas noches las quieren?
Usted	....
Recepcionista	¿Las quieren con cama de matri- monio o con dos camas?
Usted	....
Recepcionista	Bueno, vamos a ver. Sí, el número noventa y nueve y el número cien. Tienen baño y ducha. ¿Está bien?
Usted	*(yes, fine. Thanks)* ....

b   What facilities have you got? (page 59) ....

c   What are your room numbers? ....

3
a   You want to take your car to the repair shop and you're given these directions at the *estanco* in *Calle*

Velázquez (see map of Mongoya on page 31).
Are you given the right directions? *(Programme 3)*

'De aquí, siga recto hasta los semáforos. Luego, tuerza usted a la izquierda. Siga hasta el final de la Carretera de Vigo, luego a la derecha. Tome usted la primera calle a la izquierda. El taller está al lado derecho de la calle.'

b   You've finished your business at the repair shop and want to go to the *Plaza de Toros*. You're given these directions – do they take you there?

'Al final de esta calle, a la izquierda. Luego, a la derecha, por Jarama. Al final de la Avenida, tuerza usted a la derecha, y la Plaza de Toros está a la derecha.'

4   To make a *tortilla de patatas a la española* for six (see recipe page 60), you need six eggs, an onion, half a kilo of potatoes, and some olive oil. You go to the grocer's to buy what you need. *(Programme 2)* (egg – *el huevo*; onion – *la cebolla*; potato – *la patata*; olive oil – *el aceite de oliva*).

Empleada	Buenos días. ¿Qué deseaba?
Usted	*(greet her and ask for the eggs)* ....
	....
Empleada	Sí. ¿Algo más?
Usted	*(find out if she sells potatoes)* ....
	....
Empleada	Sí, sí. ¿Cuántas quiere?
Usted	*(tell her how many you want)* ....
	....
Empleada	Muy bien. ¿Algo más?
Usted	*(has she got any olive oil)* ....
	....
Empleada	Sí, hay. ¿Cuánto quiere usted?

Usted	(you'll have half a litre) ....
	....
Empleada	¿Eso es todo?
Usted	(no, you want half a kilo of onions) ....
	....
Empleada	¿Eso es todo?
Usted	(this time, yes; you want to know how much the total is) ....
	....
Empleada	Son doscientas cincuenta y nueve pesetas en total.

What is the total?

5

a   Use the *menú del día* (below) to order a meal for four. You want garlic soup, followed by fried squid rings, with caramel custard for dessert, and so does your friend. His wife wants roast chicken, with fruit to follow, and their little boy would like chicken followed by ice cream. Two of you want beer, and the others mineral water. Call the waiter, then give the order course by course. (Use *para uno/dos* after the items to indicate how many you are ordering.)
(Programme 2)

MENÚ DEL DÍA PRECIO 240 PTAS SERVICIO E IMPUESTOS INCLUIDOS
Caldo de ave o Sopa de Ajo con huevo
Pollo asado o Calamares fritos
Helado, o Flan, Fruta del tiempo
Vino, o Cerveza, o Agua mineral
Si se agotara alguno de los platos de este menú, se sustituirá por otro de características similares

MENU OF THE DAY PRICE 240 PTAS SERVICE CHARGE AND TAXES INCLUDED
Chicken consommé or Garlic Soup with egg
Roast chicken or fried squid
Ice cream, or Caramel custard, or Fresh fruit
Wine, or Beer, or Mineral water
If any one of these dishes is no longer available, we shall offer you another similar dish

b   How much (in Spanish) does the bill come to?

....

c   On the last night of your holiday you want a
memorable Spanish meal. You've ordered a *paella* for
six people, in advance. Call the waiter and ask for it.

Usted   ....
Camarero   ¿La paella está pedida?
Usted   ....
Camarero   ¿Su nombre, por favor?
Usted   ....
Camarero   Ah, sí, muy bien.

d   After the meal you'd like coffee. Order three black
coffees and one white one. Three of you also decide
to have a brandy.

....

The remaining exercises give you a chance to test out
what you've learned in new situations.

6   In each of the following situations, you want to
find out about the possibility of doing something.
First, ask the questions. Second, choose the
appropriate answer to each question from the list
below.

a   You're in a museum. Ask the attendant if you may
smoke...
Answer...
b   You want to know if the water at the campsite is
drinkable..
Answer...
c   Ask the traffic policeman where you can park your
car..
Answer...

d   You're in the hotel and want to find out when you can have lunch. ....

Answer ....

e   You want to find out where you can buy the following: stamps; sardines; oranges; postcards; olive oil; cigarettes; bread; eggs; aspirins; chicken.

....

....

....

....

Answer ....

....

....

....

....

Answers:
a   Sí, se puede beber.
b   No, señor. Está prohibido fumar.
c   En la primera calle a la derecha se puede.
d   En la farmacia; en la tienda de ultramarinos; en un estanco; en la carnicería; en un estanco o en Correos; en la frutería; en la panadería; en la tienda de ultramarinos; en la pescadería; en un estanco. *(These need to be put in the appropriate order)*
e   Desde las dos hasta las tres y media.

7   Suggestions for further practice:

a   As you use the telephone at home, translate the numbers you dial into Spanish.

Spanish telephone numbers are quoted like this:
2567493 = 2 – 56 – 74 – 93:
dos, cincuenta y seis, setenta y cuatro, noventa y tres

7226502 = 7 – 22 – 65 – 02:
siete, veintidós, sesenta y cinco, cero dos
(The odd number – if there is one – comes at the beginning. 02 is translated as above, but 20 is *veinte*.)

b   Practise telling the time in Spanish – every time you look at your watch or the clock, say the time to yourself in Spanish.

c   As you do your shopping, give yourself directions in Spanish and say which shop you're going into.

d   When you've worked through the course, try it quickly through from the beginning again and check your progress.

Worth knowing

Accommodation

Hotel accommodation is divided into two main categories, *hoteles* and *hostales*. Hotels are classified from one star to five stars and *hostales* from one to three stars. They are allowed to charge you for breakfast whether you have it or not, and there is a surcharge of 20% if you don't have at least one main meal there. A complaints book (*un libro de reclamaciones*) is provided. Booking in advance is advisable in popular resorts and during *fiestas*.

When booking a hotel room, you might be offered the following:

   habitación interior o exterior – *interior* looks out on to an inner courtyard, while *exterior* looks out on to the hotel grounds or the street.

habitación	*con*	*baño*	room	with	bath
	sin	*ducha*		without	shower

Paradores are state-run hotels, in buildings of historical interest and in exceptionally attractive surroundings. They are very popular and it's advisable to book in advance.

Albergues are roadside hotels, also state-run. There is a varying limit on how many nights you can stay.

Camping – campsites are classed *de lujo* (luxury),
first, second or third class. Prices are government
controlled, and for camping outside an official
campsite it's worth getting permission from the
authorities and/or landowner. You are not allowed to
camp within one kilometre of an established campsite
or unduly near a road.

Banks

Changing money or travellers' cheques at a Spanish
bank is usually a two-stage process. The formalities
are completed at the desk before you go to the cashier
(*la caja*) to get your money. Sometimes you are given
a numbered disc to mark your turn in the queue and
you wait to see your number flash up on a lighted
sign or hear it called.

Eating out

Spanish menus often have a translation into English
to help you – though the standard of translation is
variable! There is considerable regional variation in
cooking, which is worth exploring.

Recipe

Tortilla de patatas a la española (for 6)
6 eggs
1 onion
$\frac{1}{2}$ kilo potatoes
olive oil
salt and pepper

Peel and thinly slice the onion and potatoes. Fry them
in the oil till soft, but not brown. Beat the eggs well
and season. Mix the fried potatoes and onion with the
beaten eggs. Pour away some of the oil, reheat the
rest, and fry the mixture until golden. To turn the
tortilla over, slide it on to a plate and put it back in the
frying pan to cook the other side in the same way. The
tortilla should be soft in the middle.

Reference section

Extra grammar notes

Adjectives generally follow the noun they qualify.
Those in *-o* change their ending to *-a* when they refer
to a feminine noun. If they end in *-e* or a consonant
they don't change.

masculine			*feminine*		
	vino	barat*o*		postal	barat*a*
un	melón	pequeñ*o*	una	habitación	pequeñ*a*
el	estanco	abiert*o*	la	farmacia	abiert*a*
este	hotel	grand*e*	esta	maleta	grand*e*
	coche	azu*l*		zona	azu*l*

In the plural adjectives add *-s* if they end in a vowel;
otherwise *-es.*

	vinos	barat*os*		postales	barat*as*
los	melones	pequeñ*os*	las	habitaciones	pequeñ*as*
unos	estancos	abiert*os*	unas	farmacias	abiert*as*
estos	hoteles	grand*es*	estas	maletas	grand*es*
	coches	azul*es*		zonas	azul*es*

They change in the same way after 'is', 'are', etc.

el	estanco banco taller	está abiert*o*	la	estación de servicio oficina de turismo farmacia	está cerrad*a*

The change in endings also applies to *¿cuánto?*

¿cuánt*os*	sellos kilos litros	quiere?	¿cuánt*as*	patatas naranjas cervezas	desea?

Verbs – Spanish verbs change their endings according to the person or things they refer to. They have been translated for you as they arise in the conversations. The words for I, you, we, etc., are often omitted. Here are a few illustrations:

¿quiere ¿desea	(usted) . . . ?	*do you want . . . ?*	(*said to*
¿prefiere (usted) . . . ?		*do you prefer . . . ?*	*one*
¿tiene (usted) . . . ?		*do you have . . . ?*	*person*)

¿quieren ¿desean	(ustedes) . . . ?	*do you want . . . ?*	(*said to*
¿prefieren (ustedes) . . . ?		*do you prefer . . . ?*	*more*
¿tienen (ustedes) . . . ?		*do you have . . . ?*	*than one* *person*)

quiero deseo	*I want . . .*
prefiero	*I prefer . . .*
tenemos	*we have . . .*
vamos	*let's go . . .*

There are also changes of ending for the past tense, future tense, etc. If you want to look further into these, we suggest you follow a more advanced course. The notes to the programmes give you all the information you need 'to get by'.

¿le gusta? and *me gusta* – change according to whether you're being asked if you like one or more than one thing:

¿le gusta	España? Madrid? la paella?	sí, me gusta no, no me gusta

literally: is Spain/Madrid/the paella pleasing to you?

¿le gustan	los españoles? las habitaciones?	sí, me gusta*n* no, no me gusta*n*

literally: are the Spanish/the rooms pleasing to you?

Numbers

These have been arranged in groups so that you can see how they relate to each other.

0 cero

1 uno/una	11 once		21 veintiuno
2 dos	12 doce	20 veinte	22 veintidós
3 tres	13 trece	30 treinta	23 veintitrés
4 cuatro	14 catorce	40 cuarenta	24 veinti-
5 cinco	15 quince	50 cincuenta	cuatro *etc.*
6 seis	16 dieciséis	60 sesenta	*but*
7 siete	17 diecisiete	70 setenta	
8 ocho	18 dieciocho	80 ochenta	31 treinta y
9 nueve	19 diecinueve	90 noventa	uno
10 diez			32 treinta y
			dos

100 cien
200 doscientos
300 trescientos
400 cuatrocientos   101 ciento uno
500 quinientos   102 ciento dos
600 seiscientos   *etc.*
700 setecientos
800 ochocientos
900 novecientos
1000 mil

33 treinta y
   tres *etc.*

and similarly
41 cuarenta y
   uno
42 cuarenta y
   dos

405 cuatro- cientos cinco
625 seiscientos veinticinco
777 setecientos setenta y siete
1978 mil novecientos setenta y ocho

hundreds end in: -*os* before masculine nouns, e.g. *doscientos litros*; -*as* before feminine nouns, e.g. *quinientas pesetas*

Days of the week

lunes	– Monday	viernes	– Friday
martes	– Tuesday	sábado	– Saturday
miércoles	– Wednesday	domingo	– Sunday
jueves	– Thursday		

Months of the year

enero	– January	julio	– July
febrero	– February	agosto	– August
marzo	– March	se(p)tiembre	– September
abril	– April	octubre	– October
mayo	– May	noviembre	– November
junio	– June	diciembre	– December

Pronunciation guide

Use this guide when you are reading through the chapters, but remember that the English equivalents given below are only an approximation. The best way to learn to pronounce Spanish is to listen to and imitate the speakers in the programmes.

Vowels in Spanish are short and crisp. They are pronounced with the mouth wider open than in English and sound the same wherever they occur in a word.

i is similar to 'i' in 'machine'	sí, vino
e is similar to 'e' in 'Edward'	Pepe, leche
a is similar to 'a' in Northern English 'lass'	adiós, basta
o is similar to 'o' in 'lock'	no, poco
u is similar to 'oo' is 'spoon'	mucho, usted
y is also like 'i' in 'machine'	y, muy

When two vowels occur together, pronounce them both   fiesta, bueno

Consonants – most of them are pronounced like their English equivalents, but there are some exceptions:

b and *v* sound the same pronounced with the lips slightly parted, similar to a soft 'b'	buenos días, banco, vino, habla, lavabo, cambiar

c before i and e, and *z* before a, o, u	similar to 'th' in 'thin'	cenar, estación mozo, plaza
c before a, o, u, and *qu* before i and e	similar to 'k' in 'kitchen'	banco, calle qué, quiere, aquí
g before i and e, and *j* before all vowels	similar to a throaty English 'h'	Gibraltar, general jamón, naranja
g before a, o, u, and *gu* before i and e	similar to 'g' in 'garden'	gasolina, luego guitarra, llegue
but *gu* before a is pronounced 'gw'		agua, guardia
r in the middle of a word is slightly rolled		señorita
r at the beginning of a word and *rr* are always strongly rolled, like a Scottish 'r'		radio carretera
ch is similar to English 'ch' in 'chocolate'		chocolate, mucho
ñ is similar to 'ni' in 'onion'		mañana, española
ll is similar to 'lli' in 'million'		calle, paella, llama
d at the end of a word is similar to 'th' in 'thin'; sometimes not pronounced at all		usted, Madrid
h is not pronounced		hotel, ahora

Stress

When the word ends in a vowel or *n* or *s,* the stress falls on the next to the last syllable	cerVEza, PLAza, turISmo, EsPAña, CALLes, TIEnen

| When the word ends in a consonant other than *n* or *s*, the stress falls on the final syllable | coÑAC, taLLER, posTAL, aparCAR |
| Otherwise a written accent shows where the stress falls. This can also denote a difference in meaning | estación, café, kilómetro, inglés sí (*yes*), si (*if*), sólo (*only*), solo (*alone*) |

Regional variations This guide gives the sounds of Castilian Spanish which is only one of the languages spoken in Spain and South America, but it will be understood nearly everywhere. There are some differences in pronunciation, particularly in Andalucía and South America. The main ones are: *c* before *i* and *e* is like English 's'; *ll* is like 's' in 'measure'; *j* is often like an English 'h'.

Key to exercises

Programa número uno

1 (a) Buenos días.   (b) Buenas tardes, María Antonia.
(c) (Hola) Buenas tardes.   (d) Buenos días. ¿Cómo está (usted)?   (e) Adiós, María Antonia (Adiós, buenas tardes.)
(f) Adiós (Adiós, buenas tardes).   (g) Buenas noches.

2 (a) No, gracias.   (b) No, gracias.   (c) No, gracias. (d) No, gracias.   (e) Sí, gracias.   (f) Sí, gracias.   (g) Sí, gracias.
(h) Sí, gracias.   (j) Sí, me gusta.   (k) Sí, me gusta mucho.
(l) No, gracias, basta.   (m) Sí, me gusta mucho.

Programa número dos

1   Buenos días. ¿Hay postales? . . . Cinco, por favor. . . . Seis sellos de diez pesetas. . . . No, gracias. ¿Cuánto es? – 85 pesetas.

2   Buenos días. ¿Hay sardinas? . . . Para ocho personas. . . . (Un poco) más, por favor. . . . Sí, vale. . . . No, gracias. ¿Cuánto es? – 125 pesetas.

3(a) correct; nueve; diez; siete; siete; seis
  (b) small; large; large; small; dear; cheap; dear; cheap; very dear; very cheap

Programa número tres

1 (a) La catedral, ¿está lejos? (b) ¿Dónde está la Avenida de
Cataluña? (La Avenida de Cataluña, ¿dónde está?) (c) La
plaza de toros, ¿está lejos? (d) ¿Dónde está el Banco Central?
(El Banco Central, ¿dónde está?) (e) El Camping Quijote,
¿está lejos? (f) ¿Dónde está la estación de servicio? (La
estación de servicio, ¿dónde está?) (g) ¿Dónde está el taller?
(El taller, ¿dónde está?)

2 (a) correct (b) La Avenida de Cataluña está aquí a la
derecha. (c) correct (d) El Banco Central está en la Calle de
Valladolid, a la derecha. (e) ¿El Camping Quijote? Sí, está
lejos. (Sí, está un poco lejos.) (f) La estación de servicio está
aquí a la izquierda. (g) (Siga) recto, luego la primera a la
derecha, y la primera a la izquierda.

3 (a) ¿(dónde hay) un buzón? . . . al lado. (b) ¿dónde está la
Plaza Mayor? . . . al final (c) la oficina de turismo? . . . al
final (d) ¿(dónde hay) un café? . . . al otro lado (e) ¿(dónde
está) la farmacia? . . . en

Programa número cuatro

1 (a) correct (b) Está abierta por la mañana. (or No está cerrada
por la mañana.) (c) correct (d) correct (e) Está cerrada
por la noche. (or No está abierta por la noche.) (f) Está abierta
desde las ocho hasta la una y media.

2 (a) A la una. (b) Hasta las tres y media. (c) A las siete y
media. (d) Hasta las diez y media.
(e) Hasta las once y media. (f) Sí, se puede.
(g) No, no se puede. (h) No, no se puede.

3 (a) Barcelona; 4.40 p.m.; 11.20 p.m.
(b) No; at 9 p.m.; at 7.50 p.m.

Programa número cinco

1 (a) Surname . . . . Christian name . . . .
Date of birth . . . . Nationality . . . .
Place of birth . . . . Address . . . .
Passport no. . . . . issued at . . . . on (date)
Visitor's signature . . . .
(c) Buenas tardes. . . . No, inglés (inglesa). . . . De (the town
where you come from). . . . (your name) Y usted, ¿cómo se
llama? . . . Encantado (encantada).

2 (a) Buenas tardes. ¿Hay habitaciones, por favor?
. . . Dos, por favor. . . . Para cuatro personas. . . .
Sí. . . . Para tres noches. . . . Una con cama de

matrimonio y una con dos camas. . . . Sí, muy bien.
Gracias.   (b) Bath and shower.   (c) Nos. 99 and 100.

3   (a) Yes.   (b) No, they take you to the Hotel España.

4   Buenos días. Seis huevos, por favor. . . . ¿Hay patatas? . . .
Medio kilo. . . . ¿Hay aceite de oliva?
. . . Medio litro. . . . No, medio kilo de cebollas. . . .
Sí, gracias. ¿Cuánto es? – 259 pesetas.

5   (a) ¡Oiga, por favor! Sopa de ajo para dos. (Luego) calamares
fritos para dos y pollo asado para dos. (Luego) flan para dos,
fruta para uno y helado para uno. Cerveza para dos (*or* dos cer-
vezas) y agua mineral para dos.   (b) Novecientas sesenta
pesetas (en total).   (c) Oiga, por favor. Una paella para seis
personas. . . . Sí (está pedida).
. . . (your name)   (d) (Por favor) café solo para tres y café con
leche para uno, y coñac para tres. (*or* Tres cafés solos, un café
con leche, y tres coñacs.)

6   (a) ¿Se puede fumar? *Answer*: No, señor. Está prohibido
fumar.   (b) ¿Se puede beber el agua? *Answer*: Sí, se puede
beber.   (c) ¿Dónde se puede aparcar? *Answer*: En la primera
calle a la derecha se puede.   (d) ¿Cuándo se puede comer?
Answer: Desde las dos hasta las tres y media.
(e) ¿Dónde se puede comprar sellos; sardinas; naranjas;
postales; aceite de oliva; cigarrillos; pan; huevos; aspirinas;
pollo? *Answers*: En un estanco o en Correos; en la pescadería;
en la frutería; en un estanco; en la tienda de ultramarinos; en un
estanco; en la panadería; en la tienda de ultramarinos; en la
farmacia; en la carnicería.

Word list

NOTE: ch, ll and ñ count as separate letters in the Spanish alphabet

A

	a *at; to*		ahí *there*
	a la derecha/izquierda		ahora *now*
	on the right/left		ahora mismo *right away*
	a las . . . *at . . . o'clock*		¿algo más? *anything else?*
	abierto,-a *open*		allí *there*
	abrir *to open*		americano,-a *American*
el	aceite *oil*		aparcar *to park*
el	aceite de oliva *olive oil*	el	apellido *surname*
	de acuerdo *(yes) of course*		aquí *here*
	adiós *goodbye*		aquí mismo *right here*
la	aduana *Customs*	el	ascensor *lift*
el	aduanero *Customs officer*	la	aspirina *aspirin*
el	agua *water*	el	autobús *bus*

la avenida *avenue*
el azúcar *sugar*
azul *blue*

B

el banco *bank*
el baño *bath*
barato,-a *cheap*
basta *(that's) enough*
beber *to drink*
bien *well; good*
el bistec *steak*
blanco,-a *white*
buenas noches *goodnight*
¡buena suerte! *good luck*
buenas tardes *good afternoon/evening*
bueno,-a *good*
buenos días *good morning*
el buzón *postbox*

C

cada *each*
el café *café; coffee*
el café solo *black coffee*
la calle *street*
la cama *bed*
la cama de matrimonio *double bed*
el camarero *waiter*
cambiar *to change*
el camping *campsite*
la carnicería *butcher's*
caro,-a *dear, expensive*
la carretera *main road*
la carta *list of dishes, a letter*
la catedral *cathedral*
la cena *dinner*
la cebolla *onion*
cenar *to have dinner*
el centro *centre*
cerca *near(by)*
cerrado,-a *closed*
cerrar *to close*
la cerveza *beer*
cierto *certainly*
el cigarrillo *cigarette*
la ciudad *city; town*

el coche *car; coach*
comer *to eat; to have lunch*
la comida *lunch*
¿cómo? *pardon?*
¿cómo está (usted)? *how are you?*
¿cómo se llama? *what is your name?*
comprar *to buy*
con *with*
el coñac *brandy, cognac*
Correos *Post Office*
¿cuándo? *when?*
¿cuánto (es)? *how much (is it)?*
¿cuántos,-as? *how many?*
el cuarto *quarter*
. . . menos cuarto *quarter to . . .*
. . . y cuarto *quarter past*
la cuenta *bill*
cuesta *(it) costs*

D

de *of; from*
de acuerdo *(yes) of course*
de nada *that's all right*
la derecha *right*
desayunar *to have breakfast*
el desayuno *breakfast*
desde *from*
¿desea? *do you want?; would you like?*
deseo *I want; I would like*
despacio *slowly*
después *after; then*
la dirección *address*
¿dónde? *where?*
la ducha *shower*

E

el *the(m)*
la empleada *employee,*

el empleado *assistant*
en *in*
en total *altogether*
encantado,-a *pleased (to meet you)*
la ensalada *salad*
es *(it) is; (you) are*
eso *that*
España *Spain*
español,-a *Spanish*
está *(it) is; (you) are*
la estación de servicio *petrol station*
están *(they) are; (you) are (plural)*
el estanco *tobacconist's*
éste *this one*
este,-a *this*
exp. – expedido *issued*

F

la farmacia *chemist's*
la fecha (de nacimiento) *date (of birth)*
la ficha *registration card*
la fiesta *holiday*
al final (de) *at the end (of)*
la firma *signature*
la fruta *fruit*
la frutería *fruit shop*
fumar *to smoke*
no funciona *(it) is not working*

G

el garaje *garage*
la gasolina *petrol*
la gasolinera *petrol station*
gracias *thank you*
grande *large*
¿le gusta (n)? *do you like it (them)?*
me gusta(n) *I like it (them)*

H

la habitación *room*
¿habla? *do you speak?*
hablo *I speak*
hasta *until*
hasta luego *see you later*
hasta mañana *see you tomorrow*
hay *there is; there are*
el helado *ice cream*
hola *hello*
el hotel *hotel*
hoy *today*
el huevo *egg*

I

incluido *included*
Inglaterra *England*
inglés,-a *English*
la izquierda *left*

J

el jamón *ham*

K

el kilo *kilo(gram)*
el kilómetro *kilometre*

L

la *the (f)*
al lado *next door*
al lado de *beside; next to*
el lavabo *toilet*
¿le gusta? *do you like it?*
le *to you*
la leche *milk*
lejos *far (away)*
el limón *lemon*
el litro *litre*
lo siento *I'm sorry*
Londres *London*
luego *then*
el lugar *place*

LL

llama: ¿cómo se llama? *what is your name?*
llega *(it) arrives*
lleno,-a *full; "fill her up"*

M

la maleta *suitcase*
la manzana *apple*
 mañana *tomorrow*
la mañana *morning*
 más *more*
 más o menos *more or less*
 me, *me, to me*
 me gusta *I like it*
 me parece *I think*
 medio,-a *half*
 . . y media *half past*
el melón *melon*
 menos *less*
el menú *set meal*
el metro *metre*
el minuto *minute*
 mirar *to look at*
 mismo,-a *same*
un momento *just a moment*
el motor *engine*
el mozo *porter*
 mucho,-a *much, a lot (of)*
 muchas gracias *thank you very much*
 muy *very*
 muy bien *good, fine*

N

la naranja *orange*
 no *no*
 no funciona *(it) is not working*
la noche *night*
el nombre *name*
el número *number*

O

 o *or*
 o sea *in other words*
la oficina *office*
la oficina de turismo *tourist office*
 oiga *excuse me*
 otro,-a *other*

P

la paella *Spanish rice dish*
la página *page*

el pan *bread*
un pan *a loaf of bread*
la panadería *baker's*
 para *for*
la parada *(bus) stop*
 me parece *I think*
el pasaporte *passport*
la patata *potato*
el patio *(court)yard*
 pedido,-a *ordered*
 pequeño,-a *small*
la persona *person*
la pescadería *fishmonger's*
el pescadero *fishmonger*
la peseta *Spanish unit of currency*
el plátano *banana*
la plaza *square*
la plaza de toros *bullring*
la Plaza Mayor *main square*
un poco *a little; a bit*
el pollo *chicken*
 por *through; along*
 por ahí *that way*
 por aquí *this way; round here*
 por favor *please*
 por la mañana *in the morning*
 por la noche *at night*
 por la tarde *in the afternoon/evening*
la postal *postcard*
 prefiero *I prefer*
 presento *I introduce*
 primero,-a *first*
el programa *programme*
 prohibido *prohibited*
 ¿se puede? *can one?; is it possible?*
 pues *well; then*

Q

 que *that*
 ¿qué? *what?*
 ¿qué tal (está)? *how are you?*
 ¿quiere(n)? *do you*

want?; would you like?
quiero *I want; I would like*

R

el
la   receptionista
    receptionist
recto *straight on*
reparar *to repair*
reservar *to reserve*
el restaurante *restaurant*
el río *river*

S

sale *(it) leaves*
la sardina *sardine (fresh)*
el sello *stamp*
los semáforos *traffic lights*
señor *man; Mr*
señora *woman; Mrs, madam*
señorita *young woman; Miss*
se *one*
¿se puede? *can one?; is it possible?*
sí *yes*
si *if*
lo siento *I'm sorry*
siga *keep going*
solo *alone*
el café solo *black coffee*
sólo *only*
su *your*
super *96-octane petrol*

T

el taller *garage repair shop*
la tarde *afternoon/evening*
el taxi *taxi*
la taza *cup*
el té *tea*
el teléfono *telephone*
tenemos *we have*
la tienda *shop*

la tienda de comestibles *grocer's*
la tienda de recuerdos *souvenir shop*
la tienda de ultramarinos *grocer's*
¿tiene? *do you have?*
tienen *(they) have; (you) have (plural)*
tinto,-a *red (wine)*
todo *everything*
todo seguido *straight on*
el tomate *tomato*
la tortilla *(Spain) Spanish omelette; (South America) kind of pancake*
en total *altogether*
el tren *train*
tuerza *(you) turn*
el
la   turista *tourist*

U

un, una *a, an*
unos,-as *some*
usted (Vd.) *you (singular)*
ustedes (Vds.) *you (plural)*
la uva *grape*

V

¿vale? *is that right?/OK?*
vale *that's right/OK; (it) is worth*
vamos a ver *let's see*
varios,-as *several*
el vaso *glass*
viajar *to travel*
el viajero *visitor, traveller*
el vino *wine*

Y

y *and*
yo *I*

Z

la zapatería *shoe shop*
la zona *zone*